Paella

& other Spanish rice dishes

Paella

& other Spanish rice dishes

Louise Pickford

photography by Ian Wallace

RYLAND PETERS & SMALL

LONDON • NEW YORK

Senior Designer Sonya Nathoo
Editor Kate Eddison
Production Meskerem Berhane
Art Director Leslie Harrington
Editorial Director Julia Charles
Publisher Cindy Richards

Food and prop stylist Louise Pickford
Indexer Hilary Bird

First published in 2015
by Ryland Peters & Small,
20–21 Jockey's Fields,
London WC1R 4BW
and
341 E 116th St
New York NY 10029
www.rylandpeters.com

10 9 8 7 6 5 4 3 2 1

Printed and bound in China

Text © Louise Pickford 2015
Design and photographs © Ryland Peters
& Small 2015

ISBN: 978-1-84975-609-9

A CIP record for this book is available from the
British Library.

US Library of Congress cataloging-in-
publication data has been applied for.

Notes
• Both British (Metric) and American
(Imperial plus US cups) are included in
these recipes for your convenience, however
it is important to work with one set of
measurements and not alternate between
the two within a recipe.
• All spoon measurements are level
unless specified.
• All eggs are medium (UK) or large (US),
unless specified as large, in which case US
extra-large should be used. Uncooked or partially
cooked eggs should not be served to the very
old, frail, young children, pregnant women or
those with compromised immune systems.
• Ovens should be preheated to the specified
temperatures. We recommend using an oven
thermometer. If using a fan-assisted oven, adjust
temperatures according to the manufacturer's
instructions.

contents

introduction	6
paella	8
rice soups	24
creamy rice dishes	36
baked rice dishes	52
index	64

introduction

Rice was first introduced to Spain in the 8th century by the Arabs, and quickly became established as one of the country's most important food sources. Today Spain is the second-largest producer of rice in Europe. The variety used in paella thrives in the low-lying wetland areas of Valencia, Murcia and Catalonia.

What distinguishes these varieties of rice is their ability to absorb vast amounts of liquid (up to three times their volume). The grains swell as they cook, but retain their shape and texture. Calasparra rice is perhaps the best known outside of Spain, while bomba rice has 'Protected Designation of Origin' status, as a mark of its unique characteristics. Bomba grains are tiny and pearl-shaped, with high starch content. It is expensive and hard to find outside of Spain. If you can't find bomba or Calasparra rice, arborio rice makes a good substitute.

Traditionally, a paella should be cooked in a paella pan over an open fire, be made with bomba or Calasparra rice, and be served for large family gatherings or festivals.

Spanish rice dishes fall into four main categories determined by the volume of stock used – the more liquid, the wetter the dish. Paella or 'arroz secos' (dry rice) is always cooked in a wide, shallow pan, and left to sit for 10 minutes before serving. It should be dry on the top, crusty on the bottom, but moist in the centre.

Baked rice dishes or 'arroz al horno' are cooked in an earthenware dish called a 'cazuela' in the oven, and are similar in texture to paella. They are also left for 10 minutes before being served. You can cook all the paella recipes in the oven if you like.

Creamy rice or 'arroz en caldoso', similar to a risotto, is traditionally cooked in a pan with two handles that is deeper than a paella pan. Served as soon as it is cooked, it is accompanied by alioli, a garlicky mayonnaise.

Rice soups or 'arroz meloso' are cooked in a deep saucepan or cauldron and require the most liquid. They need to be served immediately to prevent the rice from continuing to absorb the liquid and becoming mushy.

Many varieties of fish, seafood, meat, poultry, snails and vegetables are used in Spanish rice dishes, and this varies between regions. Paella should include saffron and/or paprika, garlic, tomatoes and hot (almost boiling) stock. Stock, rather than water, is used to add flavour.

Always buy the best saffron you can afford – look for pure red strands – and grind your own saffron in a pestle and mortar rather than buying it pre-ground.

Paprika (pimentòn) is one of Spain's most highly prized commodities. There are several types including sweet, spicy and smoked. Nora peppers (pimiento choricero) are small, sweet-fleshed red/bell peppers, which are always dried. They are much more commonly used than chillies/chiles. Soak them in warm water for 15 minutes, discard the stalks, seeds and dry skin, and use the softened flesh. You can also buy ñora pepper paste, which is easier and quicker to use.

Most of the paella recipes in the book require a 35-cm/14-inch paella pan. Alternatively you can use a shallow flameproof casserole or large frying pan/skillet. I like to use less rice than is traditional, in order to balance the ingredients, allowing them to fit more easily into the pan.

Paella

valencian paella
paella valenciana

Traditionally Valencian paella includes snails, but I have omitted them; for some reason my friends tend not to eat them! If you do wish to add them, you can buy canned snails – you will find them in specialist Spanish or French food shops.

6 tablespoons olive oil
750 g/26 oz. chicken pieces, cut into small portions*
500 g/18 oz. rabbit pieces, cut into small portions*
1 large onion, finely chopped
4 garlic cloves, finely chopped
2 large ripe tomatoes, chopped
2 teaspoons sweet paprika
1/4 teaspoon saffron strands, ground
1.5 litres/6 cups hot chicken stock (see tip, page 36)
500 g/18 oz. mixed beans, such as runner beans, shelled broad/fava beans and cooked butter beans
400 g/generous 2 cups bomba, Calasparra or arborio rice
salt and freshly ground black pepper

Serves 6–8

Heat half the oil in a 40-cm/16-in. paella pan (or large, shallow, flameproof casserole). Season the chicken and rabbit pieces with salt and fry, in batches, for 5–6 minutes, until golden on both sides. Remove with a slotted spoon and set aside.

Add the remaining oil to the pan, and fry the onion and garlic for 10 minutes, until softened. Add the tomatoes, paprika and ground saffron, and cook gently for a further 5 minutes, until the mixture is almost dry. Return the meat to the pan and add the hot stock. Simmer gently for 40 minutes, until the meat is tender.

Stir in the mixed beans, then add the rice, stirring once, and return to a gentle simmer. Cook for about 20 minutes, until all the stock is absorbed and dry holes start to appear over the surface. Remove the pan from the heat but leave undisturbed for a further 10 minutes before serving.

*Tip: to cut the chicken and rabbit into small pieces it is best to use poultry shears, or perhaps you could ask your butcher to do this for you.

chicken and seafood paella
paella con pollo y marisco

This is the paella that most people know as Spanish paella, and it can be found in restaurants all over Spain, not always (in fact rarely) as the original Alicante version was intended. This adaptation is as close as I can get in a domestic kitchen. If you cannot find mussels or langoustine, use any other fresh seafood you can buy.

500 g/18 oz. mussels, cleaned
100 ml/⅓ cup dry white wine
8 large prawns/jumbo shrimp
8 langoustines (optional)
¼ teaspoon saffron strands
6 tablespoons olive oil
4 skinless chicken thigh
  fillets, quartered
350 g/¾ lb. prepared
  squid rings
4 large garlic cloves, crushed
1 red/bell pepper, seeded
  and chopped
2 tomatoes, finely chopped
1 teaspoon sweet paprika
350 g/scant 2 cups bomba,
  Calasparra or arborio rice
200 g/1⅓ cups fresh or
  frozen peas
salt and freshly ground
  black pepper
freshly chopped parsley,
  to garnish

Serves 4

Discard any mussels that do not close when tapped on the work surface. Place the mussels, still wet from cleaning, in a saucepan and place over a medium heat. Add the wine and cook the mussels, covered, for 1–5 minutes, until the shells have opened (discard any that remain closed). Strain and reserve the liquid. Set the mussels aside.

Remove the heads from the prawns/shrimp and langoustines and add the heads to the mussel liquid along with 1.25 litres/5 cups cold water. Bring to the boil, skimming the surface to remove any scum, and simmer gently for 30 minutes. Strain the stock through a fine sieve/strainer into a saucepan (you should have about 1 litre/generous 4 cups), stir in the saffron strands and keep warm.

Heat half the oil in a 35-cm/14-in. paella pan (or shallow flameproof casserole) and fry the chicken pieces for about 5 minutes, until browned. Remove with a slotted spoon and set aside. Repeat with the prawns/shrimp, then the langoustines, if using, and finally the squid rings, frying for 2–3 minutes, until golden, removing each with a slotted spoon.

Reduce the heat, add the remaining oil to the pan and gently fry the garlic for 5 minutes until softened. Stir in the pepper, tomatoes and paprika, and cook for about 5 minutes, until the sauce is sticky. Stir in the rice and return the chicken to the pan. Add the stock, bring to the boil and simmer gently for 10 minutes.

Stir in the prawns/shrimp, langoustines, mussels, squid and peas, and cook for a further 10 minutes, until the rice and seafood are cooked. Season to taste, then leave to rest for 10 minutes before serving, sprinkled with chopped parsley.

seafood paella with chorizo
paella de marisco y chorizo

In the north-west of Spain (and Portugal) chorizo sausage is added to many different dishes, and it is often combined with seafood in paella. This adds a real depth of flavour to the dish, and you can use either a mild or spicy sausage, depending on personal preference – I like the spicy variety best.

1/4 teaspoon saffron strands
500 g/18 oz. baby clams
250 g/9 oz. mussels
900 ml/scant 4 cups hot chicken stock
3–4 tablespoons olive oil
250 g/9 oz. spicy chorizo, thickly sliced
4 strips of pork belly, cut into 3-cm/1 1/4-in pieces
250 g/9 oz. large prawns/ jumbo shrimp, washed and heads removed
2 large garlic cloves, crushed
2 ripe tomatoes, finely chopped
350 g/scant 2 cups bomba, Calasparra or arborio rice
salt and freshly ground black pepper

Serves 4

Heat the saffron strands in a small dry frying pan/skillet until lightly toasted. Set aside. Scrub the clams and mussels and rinse well, discarding any that do not close when tapped on the work surface. Transfer them to a large saucepan and add a splash of water. Cook, covered, over a high heat for 3–4 minutes, until the shells have opened (discard any that remain closed). Strain the shellfish liquid into the stock and stir in the toasted saffron. Set the clams and mussels to one side.

Heat half the oil in a 30-cm/12-in. paella pan (or shallow flameproof casserole) and fry the chorizo over a medium heat until golden and the fat is released. Remove with a slotted spoon and set aside. Repeat with the pork belly and fry for 2–3 minutes, then remove and set aside. Sear the prawns/shrimp for 1 minute on each side, until golden, adding more oil as necessary. Remove and set aside.

Lower the heat and gently fry the garlic in the pan for 5 minutes. Stir in the tomatoes and cook over a medium heat for 5 minutes, until the sauce is quite dry. Return the pork pieces to the pan with the stock, bring to the boil and then stir in the rice and a little salt and pepper. Simmer gently for 15 minutes. Stir in the prawns/shrimp, clams and mussels, and simmer for a further 10 minutes, until the rice is al dente and the prawns/shrimp are cooked. Leave to rest for 10 minutes before serving.

rice with langoustine
paella con langostinos

Classically this luxurious paella would be served with whole langoustines arranged over the rice. I prefer to use the heads and claws to add flavour to the stock, and the halved langoustines are then added to the rice, making them far easier to eat. With strips of piquillo peppers and the pink shellfish, this still looks wonderful as it's brought to the table. You could use large prawns/jumbo shrimp instead.

1.25 litres/generous 5 cups fish stock (see tip, page 44)
20 large langoustines
¼ teaspoon saffron strands
6 piquillo peppers (see intro, page 35)
6 tablespoons olive oil
1 small onion, finely chopped
4 garlic cloves, crushed
grated zest and freshly squeezed juice of ½ lemon
2 tomatoes, finely chopped
1 teaspoon sweet paprika
350 g/scant 2 cups bomba, Calasparra or arborio rice
2 tablespoons freshly chopped parsley, to garnish
salt and freshly ground black pepper

Serves 4

Place the stock in a large saucepan. Remove the heads and claws from the langoustines and add to the pan. Bring to the boil and simmer gently for 20 minutes, then strain and discard the shells. Add the saffron strands to the stock and set aside to infuse. Finely chop 1 of the piquillo peppers, and cut the rest into thick strips. Set aside.

Cut the langoustine bodies in half lengthways and discard the black intestinal tract. Heat half the oil in a 35-cm/14-in. paella pan (or shallow flameproof casserole) and fry the langoustines, in batches, for 30 seconds on each side, until lightly golden. Remove with a slotted spoon and set aside.

Add the remaining oil to the pan and gently fry the onion, garlic and lemon zest for 10 minutes, until soft and lightly golden. Add the chopped peppers, tomatoes and paprika, and cook for a further 10 minutes, until the sauce is dry.

Add the rice, stir well and then pour in the stock. Cook for 15–18 minutes and then arrange the langoustine halves and pepper strips over the rice. Squeeze over the lemon juice, and cook for a further 5 minutes. Leave to rest for 10 minutes before serving, sprinkled with chopped parsley, and accompanied by some salad leaves, if you like.

paella arancini with romesco sauce
arancini de paella con salsa romesco

2 tablespoons olive oil
4 garlic cloves, crushed
1 tomato, finely chopped
1 teaspoon sweet paprika
200 g/7 oz. cooked, peeled
   prawns/shrimp, finely
   chopped
200 g/generous 1 cup bomba,
   Calasparra or arborio rice
600 ml/2½ cups hot chicken
   stock (see tip, page 36)
3 eggs
4–6 tablespoons plain/
   all-purpose flour
100 g/1¼ cups dried
   breadcrumbs
salt and freshly ground
   black pepper

romesco sauce
1 tablespoon each blanched
   almonds and blanched
   hazelnuts, roughly chopped
5 tablespoons extra virgin
   olive oil
2 large garlic cloves, chopped
1 ripe tomato, diced
1 small slice of bread, about
   25 g/1 oz., crusts removed
1 roasted red/bell pepper from
   a jar, about 100 g/3½ oz.
1 tablespoon red wine vinegar
¼ teaspoon Espelette pepper*
sunflower oil, for deep frying

Makes 16 croquettes

Similar to Italian arancini, these deep-fried paella balls are lovely as an appetizer or tapas served with the wonderfully piquant romesco sauce. This version uses paella with prawns/shrimp, but any type of paella (without any bones or shells) could be used in the same way.

Heat the oil in a 25-cm/10-in. paella pan (or shallow flameproof casserole) and fry the garlic over a low heat for 5 minutes until softened. Add the tomato, paprika and a little salt and black pepper, and cook for 5 minutes. Stir in the prawns/shrimp, then the rice. Add the stock, bring to the boil and simmer gently for 20 minutes, until the rice is al dente and the stock absorbed. Let cool, then chill the paella for 1 hour.

Meanwhile, make the sauce. Gently fry the almonds and hazelnuts in 2 tablespoons of the oil until golden, then remove with a slotted spoon. Add the garlic to the pan and fry for 5 minutes, until soft, then add the tomato and cook for a further 5 minutes. Transfer the tomato mixture to a blender or food processor, add the nuts, bread and red/bell pepper, and blend until smooth. Gradually whisk in the remaining oil and the vinegar to make a smooth sauce. Add the Espelette pepper and some salt to taste.

Beat one of the eggs and work into the chilled rice mixture until combined. Shape into 16 balls about the size of golf balls. Beat the two remaining eggs and place in a shallow dish. Dust each ball lightly with flour, dip into the egg and then coat with breadcrumbs.

Put some sunflower oil in a wok or old saucepan to about 5 cm/2 in. in depth. Heat it until a cube of bread added to the oil crisps in 20 seconds, then add the balls a few at a time, and fry for 4–5 minutes, turning halfway through, until golden brown. Drain on paper towels and repeat with the remaining balls. Serve with the romesco sauce.

* Espelette pepper is a type of pepper grown in the commune of Espelette in Basque, south-west France. It has replaced black pepper in Basque cooking. It is particularly mild with a hint of smoke and sweetness. You can use a small pinch of cayenne instead.

paella with artichokes and broad beans
paella de alcachofas y habas

Driving around the coastal regions of Spain in summer you see fields of artichokes everywhere, so it's hardly surprising to find a rice dish dedicated to this striking vegetable. You really do need to use fresh artichokes here. I have adapted this recipe to include chopped mint and, unusually for paella, to serve it with saffron alioli – it just seems to work.

4 medium artichokes, halved
  or quartered
1 lemon, halved
4 tablespoons extra virgin
  olive oil
2 bay leaves, bruised
4 garlic cloves, crushed
1 onion, finely chopped
1.2 litres/5 cups hot
  vegetable stock (see tip,
  page 60)
250 g/2 cups shelled and
  peeled broad/fava beans
350 g/scant 2 cups bomba,
  Calasparra or arborio rice
2 tablespoons freshly
  chopped mint
salt and freshly ground
  black pepper
saffron alioli, to serve
  (see tip, page 20)

Serves 4

Start by preparing the artichokes. Cut the stems off to about 2 cm/¾ in. and the leaves down to about 3–4 cm/1¼–1½ in. from the top. Peel away and discard any tough leaves to reveal the round base. In the centre there will be a hairy 'choke'. Scoop this out and discard it. Cut the bases in half and put them into a bowl filled with cold water. Squeeze in the juice from both lemon halves, and put the squeezed halves in the water too.

Heat the oil in a 35 cm/14 in. paella pan (or shallow flameproof casserole) and add the bay leaves. Fry gently for about 30 seconds, until fragrant, and then stir in the garlic, onion and a little salt and pepper. Lower the heat and cook for 20 minutes, until the onion is caramelized. Add the artichoke halves and stock, bring to the boil and simmer gently for 10 minutes.

Stir in the broad/fava beans, rice and mint, and simmer gently for 20 minutes, until the rice is al dente and the liquid absorbed. Let sit for 10 minutes before serving with a bowl of saffron alioli.

Tip: to make individual paella, follow the above method until you have added all the ingredients except the alioli. Combine everything and then divide between 4 individual pans. Bake in a preheated oven 200°C (400°F) Gas 6 for about 20 minutes, until the rice is cooked.

2 tablespoons olive oil, plus
    extra for brushing
I small onion, finely chopped
4 garlic cloves, crushed
100 g/3½ oz. smoked bacon,
    finely diced
2 tomatoes, finely chopped
I teaspoon sweet paprika
250 g/generous 1¼ cup
    bomba, Calasparra or
    arborio rice
600 ml/2½ cups hot chicken
    stock (see tip, page 36)
I egg, beaten
salt and freshly ground
    black pepper
fresh avocado, and a tomato
    and mesclun salad, to serve

alioli
3 egg yolks
2–4 garlic cloves, crushed
2 teaspoons white wine
    vinegar or lemon juice
½ teaspoon Dijon mustard
150 ml/⅔ cup fruity extra
    virgin olive oil
150 ml/⅔ cup olive oil
salt and ground white pepper

spicy chilli/chili oil
2 tablespoons extra virgin
    olive oil
a few drops of Tabasco sauce

Serves 4

fried paella with alioli
arroz frito con alioli

This is another great way to use up leftover paella (or, alternatively, prepare the rice as follows) by adding beaten egg, shaping the rice mixture into 'cakes' and frying on a flat griddle. I like to serve this for brunch with a drizzle of spicy oil, avocado, alioli and salad leaves.

Heat the oil in a large frying pan/skillet and fry the onion, garlic, bacon and a little salt and pepper for 10 minutes, until the onion is softened. Stir in the tomatoes and paprika, and cook for a further 5–10 minutes, until the mixture is dry. Stir in the rice to coat the grains and then add the stock. Simmer gently for about 20 minutes, until the rice is al dente. Remove from the heat and let cool.

To make the alioli, place the egg yolks, garlic, vinegar, mustard and a little salt and pepper in a bowl, then, using an electric hand-held whisk, whisk until the mixture is frothy. Very gradually, whisk in the two oils, a little at a time, whisking well after each addition, until the sauce is thickened and glossy, and all the oil is incorporated. If the mixture is too thick, thin it with 1–2 teaspoons boiling water, adding it gradually until you reach the required consistency.

When the rice mixture is cold, beat in the egg. Using wet hands, form the mixture into 8 flat cakes. Brush the cakes with oil and cook on a hot flat griddle or heavy frying pan/skillet for 5 minutes on each side, until browned and heated through. Keep warm.

To make the spicy chilli/chili oil, combine the extra virgin olive oil with a little Tabasco. Arrange the paella cakes on serving plates, spoon on a little alioli, top with sliced avocado, and a tomato and mesclun salad. Serve drizzled with the chilli oil.

Tip: the recipe for alioli makes a large amount and can be stored, covered with clingfilm/plastic wrap, in the refrigerator for 3–4 days. To make saffron alioli, simply add a large pinch of saffron strands to the egg yolks and garlic.

vegetable paella from murcia
paella hortelana

25 g/scant ¼ cup blanched almonds

4 tablespoons roughly chopped parsley

4 garlic cloves

6 tablespoons extra virgin olive oil

750 g/26 oz. baby vegetables, such as carrots, turnips, fennel, courgettes/zucchini and green beans

1 litre/generous 4 cups hot vegetable stock (see tip, page 60)

150 g/1¼ cup fresh or frozen peas (thawed if frozen)

1 large leek, trimmed and thinly sliced

1 green/bell pepper, seeded and finely chopped

1 plum tomato, peeled and finely chopped

2 teaspoons sweet paprika

¼ teaspoon saffron strands, ground

350 g/scant 2 cups bomba, Calasparra or arborio rice

salt and freshly ground black pepper

courgette/zucchini flowers, sliced, to garnish (optional)

Serves 4–6

Murcia, as well as producing some of the area's best rice, is also the market garden of Spain, which explains why this paella is often known simply as 'paella hortelana' meaning 'paella of the vegetable garden'. Interestingly, this dish often has a pesto-like sauce added to it, made with ground almonds, garlic and parsley. I like to use a selection of baby vegetables, but really any vegetable works well.

Toast the almonds in a dry frying pan/skillet until dotted brown, then pound them in a pestle and mortar (or use a food processor) with the parsley and 2 of the garlic cloves, until finely ground. Stir in 2 tablespoons of the oil. Set aside.

Trim the baby vegetables and halve any larger ones. Bring the stock to a boil and blanch the prepared baby vegetables and the peas for 1–3 minutes, depending on their size. Reserve the stock.

Heat the remaining oil in a 35-cm/14-in. paella pan (or shallow flameproof casserole). Crush the remaining garlic and add it to the pan with the leek, green/bell pepper and some salt and pepper. Fry gently for 10 minutes, until lightly golden. Add the tomato, paprika and ground saffron, and cook for a further 8–10 minutes, until the sauce is dry and sticky.

Stir the rice and parsley pesto into the pan, until the rice grains are well coated. Pour in the reserved stock, bring to the boil and simmer gently for 15 minutes, then stir in the blanched vegetables and continue to cook for a further 5–8 minutes, until the rice is al dente, the stock absorbed and the vegetables are tender. Season with salt and pepper. Leave to sit for 10 minutes before serving. Garnish with sliced courgette/zucchini flowers, if you like.

Rice soups

rice soup with chicken and peppers
arroz con pollo y pimientos

This is a soupy rice dish made with sweet red romano peppers. If you can find these elongated sweet peppers with pointed tips, use them, or you can use the more common bell pepper.

6 tablespoons olive oil

500 g/18 oz. chicken thighs, halved (see tip, page 8)

1 onion, finely chopped

1 large red/bell pepper (or 2 small), seeded and sliced

2 ripe tomatoes, diced

100 ml/generous 1/3 cup dry white wine

1.5 litres/generous 6 cups hot chicken stock (see tip, page 36)

1/4 teaspoon saffron strands, ground

4 tablespoons roughly chopped parsley

3 garlic cloves, peeled

250 g/generous 1 1/4 cups bomba, Calasparra or arborio rice

salt and freshly ground black pepper

Serves 4-6

Heat 2 tablespoons of the oil in a saucepan, season the chicken with salt and pepper, and add to the oil. Brown on all sides for 5 minutes, then remove with a slotted spoon and set aside.

Add 2 tablespoons more oil to the pan and fry the onion and red/bell pepper for 5 minutes. Add the tomatoes and wine, and simmer for a further 5 minutes. Return the chicken to the pan, and add the stock and ground saffron. Bring to the boil, then simmer gently for 15 minutes.

Pound the parsley and garlic together using a pestle and mortar, and stir in the remaining oil to make a paste. Stir half the parsley mix into the pan along with the rice. Simmer gently, uncovered, for about 15 minutes, until the rice is cooked. Season to taste, then serve immediately with the extra parsley garlic paste.

mallorcan 'dirty' rice
arroz brut

1 teaspoon each salt and
   ground black pepper
1/2 teaspoon each ground
   cinnamon and cloves
a little freshly grated nutmeg
1/4 teaspoon saffron
   strands, ground
6 tablespoons olive oil
2 chicken thighs, halved
   (see tip, page 8)
2 pork belly strips, roughly
   chopped, about 250 g/9 oz.
1 small onion, finely chopped
3 garlic cloves, crushed
2 ripe tomatoes, diced
1.25 litres/generous 5 cups
   hot chicken stock (see tip,
   page 36)
125 g/4 1/2 oz. chicken livers,
   chopped (optional)
1 tablespoon freshly
   chopped parsley
100 g/1 1/2 cups button
   mushrooms, halved
100 g/3/4 cup French
   beans, chopped
100 g/2 2/3 cups frozen
   peas, thawed
150 g/generous 3/4 cup bomba,
   Calasparra or arborio rice

Serves 4

It is the combination of different spices that gives this Mallorcan soup its rather worrying name, but don't be discouraged; it tastes wonderful. It is, of course, the spices that also give the soup its flavour, quite unusual in Spanish dishes but points to its Moorish origin.

Start by combining the salt, pepper, cinnamon, cloves, nutmeg and saffron in a small bowl, and set aside.

Heat half the oil in a saucepan and, when hot, fry the chicken and pork for 5 minutes, until evenly browned. Remove with a slotted spoon and set aside.

Add the remaining oil to the pan and gently fry the onion, 2 of the garlic cloves and the spice mixture for 10 minutes. Return the chicken and pork to the pan. Stir in the tomatoes and stock, bring to the boil and simmer gently for 30 minutes.

Combine the remaining crushed garlic clove with the chicken livers (if using) and parsley. Stir into the soup with the mushrooms, beans, peas and rice. Cook for a further 15 minutes until the rice is just tender. Serve immediately.

valencian rice with turnips and beans
arroz con nabos y judias blancas

If you drive through the rice fields surrounding Lake Albufera on the outskirts of Valencia, you will come across lots of small restaurants all vying for custom. This soup is typical of the area and the recipe here was given to us by our host, Jose – thank you.

500 g/18 oz. uncooked, smoked gammon knuckle/ham hock

2 bay leaves

100 g/generous $\frac{1}{2}$ cup dried haricot/navy beans, soaked in cold water for 12 hours

4 tablespoons olive oil

250 g/9 oz. small turnips, quartered or diced

250 g/9 oz. carrots, diced

4 garlic cloves, left whole

2 teaspoons ñora pepper paste (optional)*

2 teaspoons smoked paprika

$\frac{1}{4}$ teaspoon saffron strands

150 g/generous $\frac{3}{4}$ cup bomba, Calasparra or arborio rice

250 ml/generous 1 cup passata/strained tomatoes

4 small black pudding/blood sausages, about 200 g/7 oz.

salt

freshly chopped parsley, to garnish

Serves 4–6

Put 2 litres/8$\frac{1}{2}$ cups cold water into a large saucepan with the gammon knuckle/ham hock and bay leaves. Bring to the boil, straining off any scum, and simmer for about 30 minutes.

Drain the soaked beans and add them to the pan. Bring to the boil and simmer for a further 45 minutes, until the beans are cooked. Remove the gammon, finely shred the meat and discard the bone.

Heat the oil in a clean saucepan and gently fry the turnips, carrots, garlic and a little salt for 10 minutes. Stir in the ñora paste, if using, and the paprika and saffron, and cook for 1 minute. Stir in the rice.

Add the bean cooking liquid, passata/strained tomatoes, cooked beans, black pudding/blood sausage and the shredded meat, bring to the boil and simmer gently for 15 minutes, or until the rice is al dente. Serve garnished with chopped parsley.

* Tip: ñora pepper paste is made from dried ñora peppers (see page 7). This paste is a great shortcut; rather than soaking the dried pepper, you can add the prepared paste immediately. It is available from good Spanish food stores or online.

spinach, rice and bean soup
sopa con arroz, espinacas y judias blancas

I like to serve this wintery soup with chargrilled sourdough rubbed with garlic and a halved tomato - a traditional Spanish side dish known as *pan con tomate*. You can allow dinner guests to rub their toasted bread with the garlic and tomato halves themselves, if you like.

2 tablespoons extra virgin olive oil, plus extra to serve

125 g/4 1/2 oz. diced pancetta or bacon

1 onion, finely chopped

2 garlic cloves, crushed

1 tablespoon freshly chopped rosemary

grated zest and freshly squeezed juice of 1/2 lemon

150 g/generous 3/4 cup bomba, Calasparra or arborio rice

400-g/14-oz. can haricot/navy beans, drained

1.5 litres/generous 6 cups hot chicken stock (see tip, page 36)

350 g/3/4 lb. spinach

tomato bread

6 slices sourdough bread

2 tablespoons extra virgin olive oil

1 garlic clove, peeled

3 tomatoes, halved

salt and freshly ground black pepper

Heat the oil in a large saucepan and fry the pancetta for 5 minutes, until golden. Add the onion, garlic, rosemary and lemon zest to the pan with a little salt and pepper, and fry gently for 5 minutes, until the onion is softened. Stir in the rice and beans, and add the stock. Bring to the boil and simmer gently for 15 minutes.

Meanwhile wash and dry the spinach leaves, discarding any thick stalks. Shred the leaves. Stir the spinach into the soup with the lemon juice and cook for a further 5 minutes until the rice is cooked and the spinach wilted.

Meanwhile, make the tomato bread. Brush the sourdough slices with a little oil and cook on a ridged griddle until toasted on both sides. Rub all over with the garlic clove, then rub the cut side of the tomatoes over the toast and season.

Season the soup to taste, drizzle over a little olive oil and serve immediately with the tomato bread.

Serves 6

clam soup
arroz caldoso con almejas

Many years ago I was eating at a small restaurant near the port in Palma, Majorca, where I sampled a simple, but nonetheless delicious clam stew. It is the inspiration for this soup, in which I have used rice instead of beans. To clean clams, soak them in cold water with a little bran or wheat germ for an hour or so before cooking.

1 kg/2¼ lb. small clams, scrubbed

1.25 litres/generous 5 cups fish or vegetable stock (see tip, page 44)

3 tablespoons extra virgin olive oil, plus extra to serve

150 g/5½ oz. pancetta or smoked bacon, diced

1 small onion, chopped

2 garlic cloves, chopped

1 tablespoon chopped rosemary

400-g/14-oz. can chopped tomatoes

2 teaspoons hot paprika

150 g/generous ¾ cup bomba, Calasparra or arborio rice

1 bay leaf

2 tablespoons freshly chopped parsley

salt

Serves 4

Wash the clams and place them in a pan with just the water that remains on the shells. Cover and cook the clams over a medium heat for 4–5 minutes, until all the shells have opened (discard any that remain closed). Strain the clam cooking liquid into the stock and warm the stock through.

Meanwhile, heat the oil in a saucepan and fry the pancetta for 5 minutes, until browned. Add the onion, garlic, rosemary and a little salt to the pan and fry for 5 minutes, until lightly golden. Add the tomatoes and paprika, and fry gently for a further 10 minutes, until the sauce is quite dry.

Stir the rice into the pan to coat the grains and add the stock and bay leaf. Bring to the boil, and simmer gently for 15 minutes. Stir in the clams and heat through for 5 minutes. Sprinkle with chopped parsley and serve with some crusty bread.

seafood rice soup
arroz caldoso de marisco

I simply can't get enough piquillo peppers – these little pointed chilli/chile peppers are grown in pots in northern Spain, near the town of Lodosa. They are just 7.5 cm/ 3 in. in length, and are roasted over embers, giving them a sweet, smoky flavour. They are often stuffed and served as tapas, but I love the piquant flavour they add to this dish. They can be found in jars from large supermarkets or specialist food stores.

4 large langoustines
350 g/³⁄₄ lb. prawns/shrimp, peeled
1.5 litres/generous 6 cups hot fish stock (see tip, page 44)
6 tablespoons olive oil
100 g/3¹⁄₂ oz. spicy chorizo, chopped
250 g/9 oz. prepared squid rings
1 small onion, finely chopped
4 garlic cloves, crushed
2 tomatoes, finely chopped
50 g/2 oz. piquillo peppers, finely chopped
1 teaspoon sweet paprika
¹⁄₄ teaspoon saffron strands, ground
150 g/generous ³⁄₄ cup bomba, Calasparra or arborio rice
salt

Serves 4

Prepare the seafood. Cut the heads from the langoustines and prawns/shrimp and reserve. Cut the langoustine bodies in half and discard the black intestinal vein. Cut down the back of each prawn/shrimp and discard the black intestinal vein.

Bring the fish stock to the boil, add the langoustine and prawn/shrimp heads, and simmer gently for 30 minutes, skimming the surface when needed. Strain the stock into a clean pan and keep hot.

Heat half the oil in a saucepan and fry the chorizo for 3–4 minutes, until crisp and golden. Remove with a slotted spoon and set aside. Add the langoustines to the pan and stir-fry for 1 minute, until golden. Remove and set aside. Repeat with the prawns/shrimp, and then the squid.

Add the remaining oil to the pan and fry the onion, garlic and a little salt for 10 minutes, until soft and golden. Stir in the tomatoes, piquillo peppers, paprika and saffron. Cook for 5–6 minutes, until the sauce is quite dry.

Add the rice, stir well and pour in the hot stock. Return to the boil and simmer gently for 10–15 minutes. Add the langoustine, prawns and squid and cook for a further 5 minutes, until the rice is tender and the shellfish are cooked. Spoon into bowls and sprinkle over the crispy chorizo. Serve with some crusty bread.

Creamy rice dishes

rice with duck and artichokes
arroz caldoso de pato y alcachofas

In spring and late summer migrating birds, including ducks, can be found in large numbers at Lake Albufera outside Valencia, in the heart of the rice fields. They make a lovely rich addition to local rice dishes, complemented by artichokes. It is fine to use canned artichokes here.

4 confit duck legs (about 300 g/10½ oz. each)
2 tablespoons olive oil
1 onion, finely chopped
4 garlic cloves, crushed
4 tablespoons canned tomato pulp or chunky passata/strained tomatoes
1 teaspoon sweet paprika
1.25 litres/generous 5 cups hot chicken stock*
400-g/14-oz. can artichoke hearts, drained and halved
4 tablespoons freshly chopped parsley
350 g/scant 2 cups bomba, Calasparra or arborio rice
salt

Serves 4

Wipe away and discard the duck fat from the legs. Heat the oil in a flameproof casserole and gently fry the onion and garlic for 10 minutes, until softened. Stir in the tomato pulp and paprika and cook for 5 minutes, until dry. Pour in the hot stock.

Stir in the artichoke hearts and rice, and arrange the duck legs in the pan, pressing down into the rice. Return to a gentle simmer and cook for about 20 minutes, until the rice is al dente and the liquid almost absorbed. Stir in the parsley and serve.

* Tip: make chicken stock with the leftover chicken carcass from a roast chicken. Simply roughly chop or separate the bones and cavity and place in a saucepan with some chopped fresh vegetables and 2 litres of cold water. Simmer for 45 minutes until the stock has a good flavour. Strain and reserve the stock.

hunter's rice
arroz de caza

500 g/18 oz. rabbit pieces,
cut into small pieces
(see tip, page 8)
3 quails, cut into quarters
6 tablespoons olive oil
500 g/18 oz. mixed
mushrooms, such as oyster,
shiitake and brown
2 large garlic cloves, crushed
1 tablespoon each freshly
chopped rosemary, sage and
thyme, plus extra to garnish
2 tablespoons blanched
hazelnuts, toasted and
ground
2 tomatoes, finely chopped
2 teaspoons hot paprika
1/4 teaspoon saffron strands,
ground
1.5 litres/generous 6 cups
hot chicken stock (see tip,
page 36)
450 g/2 1/4 cups bomba,
Calasparra or arborio rice
salt and freshly ground
black pepper

Serves 6–8

It's not hard to imagine the type of ingredients found in this aptly named dish, full of the bounty of a day's hunting, as well as ingredients such as mushrooms and herbs that can be found growing in the countryside. Here these are combined to produce an intense rice dish, ideal for a family gathering. You can use chicken or pork instead of rabbit, if you like.

Season the rabbit and quail pieces with salt and pepper.

Heat 2 tablespoons of the oil in a flameproof casserole and fry the rabbit and quail for 5–6 minutes, until golden brown. Remove with a slotted spoon and set aside.

Add 2 more tablespoons of oil and fry the mushrooms over a high heat for 3–4 minutes, then remove with a slotted spoon.

Add the remaining oil to the pan and gently fry the garlic and herbs for 5 minutes. Add the hazelnuts and cook for 5 minutes. Stir in the tomatoes, paprika and saffron, and fry for a further 5 minutes, until the sauce is dry.

Add the rabbit, quail and mushrooms to the pan, and pour in the hot stock. Bring to the boil and simmer gently for 15 minutes. Stir in the rice and simmer again for a further 15–20 minutes, until the rice is al dente. Sprinkle over some herbs and serve with some crusty bread and a crisp green leaf salad.

cuban rice
arroz cubano

This Cuban-inspired rice dish, traditionally served at breakfast, is typical of the cross migration of cuisines. The rice is flavoured with bacon and served with a tangy tomato sauce, a fried egg and fried banana! It reminds me of the Indonesian dish, nasi goreng, and it tastes fabulous. Thanks to Ruben, chef at *The Beach at Bude* in Cornwall in the south of England, for this recipe.

4 tablespoons of sunflower oil, plus extra for frying
1 onion, chopped
2 garlic cloves, finely chopped
4 tomatoes, finely chopped
1 teaspoon white wine vinegar
1 teaspoon dried oregano
2 rashers/strips bacon, chopped
250 g/generous 1 1/4 cups bomba, Calasparra or arborio rice
600 ml/2 1/2 cups hot chicken stock (see tip, page 36)
2 bananas, halved
4 tablespoons seasoned flour
4 eggs
1 tablespoon freshly chopped coriander/cilantro
salt and freshly ground black pepper
a few rocket/arugula leaves, to serve

Serves 4

Heat half the oil in a saucepan and fry the onions and garlic for 20 minutes, until caramelized, adding a little water if necessary to stop the onion burning. Stir in the tomatoes and simmer for a further 20 minutes, until the sauce is thick. Stir in the vinegar and oregano, and season to taste. Keep warm.

Heat the remaining oil in a frying pan/skillet and fry the bacon for 3–4 minutes, until golden. Stir in the rice and then add the stock. Bring to the boil and simmer gently for 20 minutes, until al dente. Keep warm.

Dust the bananas with seasoned flour and shallow fry in sunflower oil for 1–2 minutes on each side, until golden. Remove with a slotted spoon and then fry the eggs until cooked to your liking.

Arrange the rice on serving plates and top each serving with half a banana and a fried egg. Sprinkle with coriander/cilantro and serve immediately with the tomato sauce and a little rocket/arugula.

rice with lobster
arroz caldoso con langosta

Rice with lobster is typically found in most coastal towns in Spain. The texture of this version reminds me of an Italian risotto; the rice creamy but still slightly al dente. It was inspired by a recent trip to Barcelona, where we enjoyed a Catalan variation, which included ñora peppers and toasted almonds.

6 tablespoons olive oil
1 frozen raw lobster, about
  500 g/18 oz., defrosted
  and cut into pieces*
4 garlic cloves, peeled
1 small onion, very finely
  chopped
1 tablespoon roughly
  chopped parsley
1 tablespoon ñora pepper
  paste (see tip, page 28)
1/4 teaspoon saffron strands,
  ground
2 tablespoons toasted
  almonds
1 anchovy fillet, chopped
1 ripe tomato, diced
150 g/generous 3/4 cup
  bomba, Calasparra or
  arborio rice
500–600 ml/2–2 1/2 cups hot
  fish stock (see tip, page 44)
salt

Serves 2

Heat 4 tablespoons of the oil in a flameproof casserole, add the lobster pieces and stir-fry for 2–3 minutes, until golden. Remove with a slotted spoon and set aside.

Add the garlic to the pan and fry gently for 5 minutes, until really soft and golden. Add the onion to the pan, lower the heat and cook gently for 15 minutes, until soft and golden.

Add the parsley, ñora pepper paste, saffron, almonds, anchovy and tomato to the pan, and cook for a further 5 minutes, until the sauce is quite dry. Transfer to a blender and pulse to make a smooth sauce.

Add the remaining oil to the pan, add the sauce and heat through. Stir in the rice and arrange the lobster over the top. Pour in the stock and simmer gently for about 15–20 minutes, until the rice is al dente. Season with salt to taste, and serve at once.

* If you buy frozen raw lobster, defrost it thoroughly in the refrigerator. Alternatively, buy a live lobster and kill it humanely at home. Freeze the live lobster for 1 hour until it is almost comatose and still, then place it on a board and firmly insert a sharp knife into the cross on the lobster's head. Quickly split the lobster lengthways in half. To prepare the lobster, place tummy-side up on a board and, using a sharp knife, cut in half straight down through the head and body. Separate the claws and, using claw crackers (or small hammer), crack the shell lightly. Clean out the soft brown part from the head section and discard. Cut the body into 4 or 5 pieces.

rice with squid in ink
arroz negro

Black, unctuous and quite unlike any other rice dish, the flavour of this crazy-looking rice is truly fabulous. You can use either squid or cuttlefish for this recipe, and ask your fishmonger for the small packets of prepared squid ink. You will need 2 small packs or 2 teaspoons. Double the quantities, as required, for more people.

350 g/¾ lb. prepared small squid or cuttlefish (you can use pre-cleaned squid)

4 tablespoons olive oil

2 large garlic cloves, chopped

1 small red/bell pepper, seeded and diced

1 large tomato, seeded and finely chopped

1 teaspoon smoked paprika

¼ teaspoon saffron strands, ground

1 tablespoon freshly chopped parsley

2 teaspoons squid ink

500 ml/generous 2 cups hot fish or chicken stock*

150 g/generous ¾ cup bomba, Calasparra or arborio rice

salt and freshly ground black pepper

Serves 2

Roughly chop the prepared squid. Heat the oil in a 25-cm/10-in. frying pan/skillet or shallow flameproof casserole, and quickly stir-fry the squid for 2–3 minutes, until lightly golden. Remove with a slotted spoon.

Add the garlic and red/bell pepper to the pan with a little salt, and fry gently for 10 minutes, until softened. Add the tomato, paprika, saffron and parsley, and cook for a further 5 minutes, until the mixture is quite dry.

Place the squid ink in a bowl and stir in a little of the hot stock. Add the rice to the casserole, stir well and then add the squid pieces, inky stock and the rest of the stock. Stir once and then bring to the boil and simmer gently for 20 minutes, until the rice is al dente and the stock is creamy and quite sticky. Season to taste, and serve immediately with some crusty bread.

*Tip: to make fish stock, place fish trimmings and prawn/shrimp shells, etc., into a pan with some chopped celery, leek, parsley, thyme and a little salt and pepper. Add 1.5 litres/generous 6 cups cold water, bring to the boil and simmer for 30 minutes. Strain.

rice with salt cod
arroz con bacalao

Along with their love of rice, the Spanish also have a great fondness for salt cod, and it can be found in dishes all over the mainland and islands in various guises. Naturally enough, there are many recipes that combine these two favourite ingredients. You will need to begin this dish 24 hours before serving.

650–750 g/23–26 oz. salt cod

4 tablespoons olive oil

200 g/7 oz. cooked, peeled prawns/shrimp, finely chopped

4 garlic cloves, chopped

4 tomatoes, seeded and chopped

2 teaspoons ñora pepper paste (see page 28)

1 teaspoon hot paprika

300 g/generous 1 1/2 cups bomba, Calasparra or arborio rice

1 litre/generous 4 cups hot fish or chicken stock (see tips, pages 44 and 36)

75 g/1/2 cup (dark) raisins

2 tablespoons freshly chopped coriander/cilantro

1 tablespoon finely chopped preserved lemon

salt and freshly ground black pepper

Serves 4

Place the salt cod in a large bowl of cold water and leave to soak for 24 hours, stirring and changing the water as frequently as you can – perhaps 2–3 times during the day, then last thing at night and first thing the next morning. Once the cod is softened, remove it from the water, rinse it well and carefully discard any skin and bones. Thoroughly dry the pieces of fish on paper towels. Flake the flesh into bite-sized chunks (you should be left with about 400 g/14 oz.).

Heat half the oil in a non-stick, flameproof casserole and fry the fish over a medium heat for 3–4 minutes, until golden. Remove with a slotted spoon and set aside. Repeat with the prawns/shrimp. (If you do not have a non-stick casserole, fry the fish in a non-stick frying pan/skillet and transfer to a flameproof casserole. Otherwise, the fish will fall apart.) Lower the heat, add remaining oil and gently fry the garlic for 5 minutes, until soft. Add the tomatoes, ñora pepper paste and paprika, and cook over a medium heat for 10 minutes, or until the sauce is thick.

Stir the rice into the pan, add the stock, bring to the boil and simmer gently for about 15 minutes. Stir in the raisins, salt cod and prawns/shrimp, and cook for a further 5 minutes, until the rice is tender and most of the stock absorbed. Stir in the coriander/cilantro and preserved lemon, and season with salt and pepper. Serve immediately.

green rice with clams
arroz verde con almejas

This dish comes form the Basque region of Spain, where it can be made either with cooked rice, or, as it is here, with cooking the rice as part of the recipe. You could use any fresh clams for this, but small ones work particularly well.

6 tablespoons olive oil

4 garlic cloves, crushed

75 ml/5 tablespoons dry white wine

1 kg/2¼ lb. small clams

1 bunch spring onions/scallions, trimmed and finely chopped

1 green/bell pepper, seeded and diced

1 green chilli/chile, seeded and finely chopped

grated zest and freshly squeezed juice of 1 lemon

250 g/generous 1¼ cups bomba, Calasparra or arborio rice

900 ml/scant 4 cups hot fish stock (see tip, page 44)

4 tablespoons freshly chopped parsley

salt

Serves 4

Heat 2 tablespoons of the oil in a saucepan, add half the garlic and fry gently for 3–4 minutes, until soft. Add the wine and bring to the boil, then stir in the clams. Cook, covered, for 4–5 minutes, until all the clams have opened (discard any that remain closed). Strain and reserve the cooking liquid and set the clams to one side.

Heat the remaining oil in a saucepan and fry the remaining garlic, spring onions/scallions, green/bell pepper, chilli/chile and lemon zest for 5 minutes until softened.

Stir in the rice until the grains are well coated, and then add the clam liquid, stock and half the parsley. Simmer gently, uncovered, for 15 minutes.

Stir in the clams and the remaining parsley, and cook for a final 5 minutes, until the rice is al dente. Stir in the lemon juice and serve at once.

rice pudding with caramel oranges arroz con leche y naranjas caramelizadas

Rice pudding can be found in homes and restaurants all over Spain, especially in Asturias and northern areas, where dairy products are produced. Every region varies the ingredients slightly, and in the north, the dish is often flavoured with lemon and cinnamon, and enriched with egg yolks or butter. I have added my own twist with sliced oranges in syrup flavoured with Pedro Ximénez, a delicious Spanish sweet sherry. Best served at room temperature.

1.5 litres/generous 6 cups full-fat/whole milk
grated zest of 1 lemon
1 cinnamon stick, lightly bashed
150 g/generous ¾ cup bomba, Calasparra or arborio rice
75 g/6 tablespoons caster/granulated sugar
2 egg yolks

caramel oranges
4 small Valencian oranges
75 g/6 tablespoons soft light brown sugar
4 tablespoons water
2 tablespoons Pedro Ximénez (or sweet sherry)

Serves 6

Place the milk, lemon zest and cinnamon in a saucepan and bring slowly to the boil. Stir in the rice and sugar, and simmer fast for 5 minutes, then lower the heat and cook very gently, stirring from time to time, for about 45 minutes, until the rice is really soft and creamy. Discard the cinnamon stick.

Remove from the heat and let cool for 10 minutes, then beat in the egg yolks. Spoon the creamy rice into 6 glasses or dishes, and let cool. Chill until required. (You will need to return them to room temperature for 1 hour before serving.)

Meanwhile, prepare the oranges. Pare the zest of 1 of the oranges into thin strips and squeeze its juice into a small saucepan. Stir in the brown sugar and water and heat gently, stirring, until the sugar is dissolved. Stir in the shredded orange zest and simmer for about 5 minutes, until the sauce is syrupy. Remove from the heat and stir in the sherry.

Peel the remaining 3 oranges and cut them into slices. Arrange the slices in serving bowls. Pour the hot syrup over the orange slices and leave until cold.

To serve, bring the rice to room temperature for 1 hour, then serve topped with the caramel oranges.

Baked rice dishes

stuffed peppers with chorizo
pimientos rellenos de arroz con chorizo

1 tablespoon olive oil
50 g/2 oz. mild chorizo, diced
1 small onion, finely chopped
1 large garlic clove, crushed
1 teaspoon chopped thyme
1 large tomato, diced
200 g/generous 1 cup bomba,
 Calasparra or arborio rice
500 ml/generous 2 cups hot
 chicken stock (see tip,
 page 36)
4 red/bell peppers

spicy tomato sauce
400-g/14-oz. can chopped
 tomatoes
2 tablespoons olive oil
1 garlic clove, crushed
a pinch of dried chilli/
 hot pepper flakes
1/2 teaspoon caster/
 granulated sugar
salt and freshly ground black
 pepper
saffron alioli, to serve
 (see tip, page 20)

Serves 4

I would imagine that this dish was first invented to use up leftover paella, which is often cooked in large quantities. It is, however, delicious in its own right.

Preheat the oven to 200°C (400°F) Gas 4.

Start by making the sauce. Place the tomatoes, oil, garlic, chilli/hot pepper flakes, sugar and some salt and pepper in a saucepan, and bring to the boil. Simmer gently for 15–20 minutes, until thickened. Pour into a 1.5-litre/6-cup baking dish.

Heat the oil in a frying pan/skillet and gently fry the chorizo for 5 minutes, until browned. Add the onion, garlic and thyme to the pan, and fry gently for 10 minutes. Stir in the tomato and a little salt and pepper, and cook for 5 minutes. Then stir in the rice. Add the stock, bring to the boil and simmer gently for about 15–20 minutes, until the rice is al dente with just a little stickiness remaining.

Cut the tops from the red/bell peppers, reserving the lids. Scoop out the seeds and membrane. Spoon the rice mixture into the peppers and pop the 'lids' back on. Place in the dish with the sauce, cover with foil and bake for 1 hour.

Remove the foil and bake for a final 15 minutes, until charred and tender. Let cool for 30 minutes, before serving at room temperature with saffron alioli.

baked chicken and seafood rice
arroz al horno con marisco y pollo

A familiar combination in many Spanish rice dishes, any meat, including chicken, and seafood work well together. You can vary the seafood using whatever is available.

1 litre/generous 4 cups hot chicken stock (see tip, page 36)

1/4 teaspoon saffron strands

1 tablespoon lemon juice

6 tablespoons olive oil

350 g/3/4 lb. skinless chicken thighs, halved (see tip, page 8)

350 g/3/4 lb. prawns/shrimp, peeled

4 garlic cloves

2 bay leaves, crumbled

2 teaspoons sweet paprika

100 ml/generous 1/3 cup canned tomato pulp or passata/strained tomatoes

350 g/scant 2 cups bomba, Calasparra or arborio rice

150 g/1 1/4 cups frozen peas, thawed

250 g/9 oz. mussels, cleaned

250 g/9 oz. small clams, cleaned

salt and freshly ground black pepper

3 tablespoons freshly chopped parsley, to garnish

Serves 6

Preheat the oven to 180°C (360°F) Gas 4. Place the stock, saffron and lemon juice in a saucepan and bring to the boil. Keep warm.

Meanwhile, heat half the oil in a 35-cm/14-in. paella pan (or flameproof shallow casserole). Season the chicken pieces with salt and pepper, and fry over a high heat for 4–5 minutes, until golden. Remove with a slotted spoon. Repeat with the prawns/shrimp, stir-frying for 1 minute. Set aside.

Add the remaining oil to the pan, and fry the garlic, bay leaves and paprika for 5 minutes, until fragrant. Stir in the tomato pulp and cook for 5 minutes, until dry. Stir in the rice, chicken thighs and stock. Bring to the boil and cook over a low heat for 10 minutes.

Stir in the peas, prawns/shrimp, mussels and clams, pressing well down into the rice. Transfer to the oven and bake for 15 minutes, until the liquid is absorbed. Discard any mussels or clams that have not opened. Allow to rest for 10 minutes before serving garnished with parsley and accompanied by some rocket/arugula, if you like.

baked rice with lamb
arroz al horno con cordero

Although it is traditional to use both sausages and meatballs in Spanish rice dishes, this version is one I have adapted to incorporate meatballs made from merguez sausages, because they are just delicious. Simply roll the sausagemeat into balls – so quick and easy. You could also use other sausages, if you like.

500 g/9 oz. merguez sausages
8 lamb cutlets, French-
    trimmed (ask your butcher
    to do this for you)
2 teaspoons dried oregano
3 tablespoons olive oil
1 onion, finely chopped
2 garlic cloves, crushed
250 ml/generous 1 cup
    passata/strained tomatoes
1/4 teaspoon saffron strands,
    ground
600 ml/2 1/2 cups hot chicken
    stock (see tip, page 36)
75 g/1/2 cup currants or
    (dark) raisins
200 g/generous 1 cup bomba,
    Calasparra or arborio rice
2 tablespoons freshly
    chopped mint
salt and freshly ground
    black pepper

Serves 4

Preheat the oven to 200°C (400°F) Gas 6.

Remove the skin from the sausages, divide the sausage meat into 16 pieces and roll into walnut-sized balls. Set aside.

Rub the lamb cutlets with oregano, salt and pepper. Heat half the oil in a frying pan/skillet and fry the lamb for 5 minutes, until browned all over. Transfer to a plate.

Add the remaining oil to the pan and fry the sausage balls for 5 minutes, until browned. Remove with a slotted spoon and set aside.

Add the onion, garlic and a little salt and pepper to the pan, and fry gently for 10 minutes. Add the passata, saffron, stock and currants, and bring to the boil. Stir the rice and mint into the pan and simmer for 5 minutes.

Divide the rice mixture between 4 individual paella pans (or small baking dishes) and top each one with the lamb and sausage balls. Transfer to the oven and bake for about 20 minutes, until the rice is cooked and the stock absorbed.

Tip: you can make this as one large paella in a 35-cm/14-in paella pan, and continue as above, baking for a little longer, if required.

crusted rice
arroz con costra

This is an oven-baked rice dish enriched with a delicious egg crust just before serving. It originates from the Murcia region of Spain, one of the country's most important rice and vegetable growing regions. Traditionally this was cooked in a cazuela (see page 7), but a flameproof casserole works just as well.

4 tablespoons olive oil
1 head garlic, trimmed but left whole
3 chicken thighs, cut in half *
2 pork belly strips, each cut into 3 pieces (about 250 g/ 9 oz.)
2 tomatoes, diced
1 teaspoon sweet paprika
350 g/scant 2 cups bomba, Calasparra or arborio rice
100 g/3 1/2 oz. black pudding/ blood sausage
400-g/14-oz. can chickpeas, drained
1.25 litres/generous 5 cups hot chicken stock (see tip, page 36)
6 eggs, beaten
salt and freshly ground black pepper

Serves 6

Preheat the oven to 200°C (400°F) Gas 6.

Heat the oil in a flameproof casserole and fry the whole garlic head for 5 minutes, until evenly browned. Add the chicken thighs and pork belly, and fry for 5 minutes, until browned. Remove the meat from the pan with a slotted spoon and set aside.

Add the tomatoes and the paprika to the pan (the garlic can stay in) and cook gently for 5 minutes, then stir in the rice so all the grains are coated.

Arrange the chicken, pork and the black pudding/blood sausage in the pan, with the garlic in the middle. Sprinkle over the chickpeas and pour in the stock with a little salt and pepper. Transfer to the oven and bake for 30–35 minutes, or until the liquid is absorbed.

Whisk the eggs with a little more salt. Remove the pan from the oven, carefully pour over the beaten egg and return to the oven for a further 5 minutes, or until the egg is set, forming a crust. Leave to sit for 10 minutes before serving.

*Tip: use poultry shears to cut the chicken thighs in half, or ask your butcher to do this for you.

baked rice with chickpeas and raisins
arroz al horno con garbanzos y pasas

It is hardly surprising to find Moorish influences in many of Spain's rice dishes, as it was the Moors who first introduced rice to Spain in the 8th century. Here rice is combined with chickpeas and raisins, as is typical of the sweet/savoury nature of many Moorish recipes. I also like to add a little ground cinnamon to this dish.

5 tablespoons olive oil
1 head garlic, trimmed but left whole
1 small onion, finely chopped
1 large tomato, finely chopped
1 teaspoon sweet paprika
1/2 teaspoon ground cinnamon
200 g/1 1/2 cups cooked chickpeas, drained
100 g/2/3 cup (dark) raisins
1 litre/generous 4 cups vegetable stock *
350 g/scant 2 cups bomba, Calasparra or arborio rice
salt and freshly ground black pepper
freshly chopped parsley, to garnish
saffron alioli, to serve (see tip, page 20)

Serves 4–6

Preheat the oven to 200°C (400°F) Gas 6.

Heat the oil in a flameproof casserole or cazuela (see page 7). Fry the head of garlic over a medium heat for 5 minutes, until golden. Add the onion and lower the heat, fry gently for 10 minutes, then add the tomato, paprika and cinnamon, and cook for a further 5–8 minutes, until the sauce is quite dry. Season with salt and pepper.

Stir in the chickpeas, raisins and stock, and bring to the boil. Sprinkle over the rice, stir once and return to the boil. Transfer to the oven. Bake for about 25 minutes, until the rice is al dente and the stock absorbed. Remove from the oven and leave to sit for 10 minutes before serving with the alioli.

* Tip: to make a tasty vegetable stock place roughly chopped onions, carrots, leeks, garlic, mushrooms and potatoes, as well as some roughly chopped parsley and thyme, and some salt and pepper. Add 2 litres/8 1/2 cups water and cook for 45 minutes, until the stock has taken on a good flavour. Strain and reserve the stock.

baked saffron rice pudding
arroz con leche y azafrán al horno

There is something truly comforting about eating baked rice pudding. Perhaps it's the fond memories of childhood puds, or the soft, creamy texture of the dish. This version offers an intriguing hint of saffron. If you want, you can add some dried raisins or currants before baking and serve topped with a drizzle of cream and whatever fresh fruits are in season.

125 g/scant ¾ cup bomba, Calasparra or arborio rice
1 litre/generous 4 cups full-fat/whole milk
75 g/6 tablespoons caster/granulated sugar
1 vanilla pod/bean, split
a pinch of saffron strands
25 g/2 tablespoons butter, diced
cream and seasonal fruits, to serve (optional)

Serves 4

Preheat the oven to 150°C (300°F) Gas 2 and grease a 1.5-litre/6-cup baking dish.

Wash the rice in a sieve/strainer, shake well and place in the prepared dish. Place the milk, sugar, vanilla pod/bean and saffron strands in a saucepan and bring to the boil. Remove from the heat and leave to infuse for 15 minutes.

Discard the vanilla pod/bean, scraping the seeds into the milk, then pour the milk over the rice. Bake in the preheated oven for 30 minutes.

Stir well, carefully dot the top with butter and bake for a further 1 hour, until the top of the pudding is golden brown. Lift a little of the skin with the point of a knife; the sauce should be thick and creamy. Cook for longer, if required.

Rest for 10 minutes before serving with some cream and fresh fruits, if wished.

index

alioli, fried paella with 20
arancini with romesco sauce 16
artichokes: paella with broad
    beans and 19
    rice with duck and 36

bacon: Cuban rice 40
    fried paella with alioli 20
bananas: Cuban rice 40
beans: spinach, rice and bean
    soup 31
    Valencian paella 8
    Valencian rice with turnips
    and beans 28
bell peppers see peppers
broad beans, paella with
    artichokes and 19

caramel oranges 51
chicken: baked chicken and
    seafood rice 55
    chicken and seafood paella 11
    crusted rice 59
    Mallorcan 'dirty' rice 27
    rice soup with chicken and
    peppers 24
    Valencian paella 8
chickpeas: baked rice with
    raisins and 60
    crusted rice 59
chorizo: seafood paella with
    12
    stuffed peppers with 52
clams: baked chicken and
    seafood rice 55
    clam soup 32
    green rice with 48
    seafood paella with chorizo
    12
crusted rice 59

Cuban rice 40
duck, rice with artichokes and
    36

eggs: Cuban rice 40

gammon: Valencian rice 28
garlic: alioli 20
green rice with clams 48

haricot beans see beans
hunter's rice 39

lamb, baked rice with 56
langoustines: rice with 15
    seafood rice soup 35
lobster, rice with 43

Mallorcan 'dirty' rice 27
Merguez sausages: baked rice
    with lamb 56
mushrooms: hunter's rice 39
mussels: baked chicken and
    seafood rice 55
    chicken and seafood paella
    11

oranges, caramel 51

paella: fried paella with alioli 20
    paella arancini with romesco
    sauce 16
    paella with artichokes and
    broad beans 19
    rice with langoustine 15
    seafood paella with chorizo
    12
    Valencian paella 8
    vegetable paella from
    Murcia 23

peppers: green rice with
    clams 48
    rice soup with chicken and
    peppers 24
    romesco sauce 16
    stuffed peppers with chorizo
    52
prawns: baked chicken and
    seafood rice 55
    paella arancini with romesco
    sauce 16
    rice with salt cod 47
    seafood paella with chorizo
    12
    seafood rice soup 35

quail: hunter's rice 39

rabbit: hunter's rice 39
    Valencian paella 8
raisins, baked rice with
    chickpeas and 60
rice pudding with caramel
    oranges 51
rice soup with chicken and
    peppers 24
rice with duck and artichokes
    36
rice with langoustine 15
rice with lobster 43
rice with salt cod 47
rice with squid in ink 44
romesco sauce 16

saffron rice pudding 63
salt cod, rice with 47
seafood: baked chicken and
    seafood rice 55
    chicken and seafood paella
    11

seafood paella with
    chorizo 12
seafood rice soup 35
shrimp see prawn
soups: clam soup 32
    Mallorcan 'dirty' rice 27
    rice soup with chicken and
    peppers 24
    seafood rice soup 35
    spinach, rice and bean soup
    31
    Valencian rice with turnips
    and beans 28
spinach, rice and bean soup 31
squid: chicken and seafood
    paella 11
    rice with squid in ink 44
    seafood rice soup 35

tomatoes: clam soup 32
    romesco sauce 16
    spicy tomato sauce 52
turnips, Valencian rice with
    beans and 28

Valencian paella 8
Valencian rice with turnips
    and beans 28
vegetable paella from Murcia
    23